PANORAMIC LOU

John Stammers studied Philosophy at King's College London
and is an Associate of King's College. He is a freelance writer.
He was born in Islington, London, where he still lives.

Panoramic Lounge-Bar

John Stammers

PICADOR

First published 2001 by Picador
an imprint of Macmillan Publishers Ltd
25 Eccleston Place London SW1W 9NF
Oxford and Basingstoke
Associated companies throughout the world
www.macmillan.com

ISBN 0 330 48076 6

1 3 5 7 9 8 6 4 2

A CIP catalogue record for this book is available from
the British Library.

Typeset by Intype London Ltd
Printed and bound in Great Britain by
Mackays of Chatham plc, Chatham, Kent

I wrote your name in the sand
the sea washed it away
I wrote your name in the sea

to my parents

CONTENTS

Acknowledgements, xi

Nom de Plume, 1

Weather Report, 2

There are some Places Beyond, 4

Breakages, 5

My Great Grandfather's
Graveplate at Gestingthorpe, 6

House on the Beach, 8

Where is the Rest of my Horse?, 11

Impression, 12

¿Que Pasa?, 13

The Wolf Man, 14

Stuck, 17

On Your Last Evening Together, 18

The Underlining of the Hemisphere, 20

The Clinic, 21

Testimony, 23

The Party, 26

Light, 27

So what do you do on your week off?, 29

I Put Away My Ears, 32

Aspects of Kees, 33

The Tell, 35

The Last Vampire, 36

Certain Sundry Matters, 37

The Infanta of Castile Rides out with Leopard,
Parrot and Mandolin, 39

Feet, 40

Listening to his Record Collection
with Roddy Lumsden, 41

Torch, 43

Spine, 45

When I' The Night, 46

Stella, 47

The Call, 49

Perhaps You Have Dreams, 51

ACKNOWLEDGEMENTS

Acknowledgements are due to the editors of the following publications in which some of these poems first appeared: *Magma*, *Papercuts*, *Poetry Review*, *Tabla*. 'The Wolf Man' was a winner of the 1999 Blue Nose Poets-of-the-year Competition and was published in the winners anthology *Before Ripening*.

Thanks are due to Michael Donaghy, Roddy Lumsden and Don Paterson for their criticism, advice and support.

NOM DE PLUME

The bunch of flowers in the vase, what *are* they called?
I'll call them Anstruthers for no other reason
than that. Someone has set them there
in a drastic tableau, an attempt to let them impose
their one iridescence on the view. Those Anstruthers,
I know I'll recall them, their fine, pointed petals like scalpels,
the way the powder and near-navy blues leak one into another
and the discreet green of their stiff stems and leaves:
I'll see them in my mind's eye (that odd concept
that always makes me feel like Cyclops). One day,
doing something quite mundane, I'll look at them
in the plastic time that holds such mementoes
and long after the implacable in-rush
of others into the room, none of whom will say,
'How beautiful the Anstruthers are, despite everything!'

WEATHER REPORT

Sea Vista fluoresces like luminous eels;
someone painted this place cream
and never touched it again.
You can't get that colour anymore,
just cream, you say;
flakes detach from the facade
and join in the general descent.

The tint of the raindrops' perpetual concerto
misses, by about none,
the lilac of the waltzes of the tea room.
So much liquid, is it all required?
Take cappuccino or lip gloss,
those suspensions of our age,
or the actual rain:
clouds (mauve semblance of what is)
accumulate as if instructed by old masters.
And when you think about it, El Greco's wrist
did live its life inches from the very threshold
                                    of creation:
the canvases like culture mediums,
spread with florets of grim hues and him
drawing out the grand designs into being
through the tip of the brush.

And, if to prove conclusively
that there is madness in Methodism,
the sign outside the mock-gothic hall says:
In the Midst of Life we are in Death
but you, you wear the ludicrous sea-side hats
of self-aggrandisement, as if the gust
that tossed the last one into the sea
was your own idea:
not content with wrapping yourself up
in love, only love, love,
you do no more than write an epigraph for us
on the back of the old hotel
with its seen better days
and panoramic lounge-bar:

THEY CAME THEY SAW THEY CAME

Ha Ha Ha, you went.
Don't perpetrate mirth like that,
you spray-can El Greco,
I said, and I noticed
the soft flesh of your wrist
and wanted you again.

THERE ARE SOME PLACES BEYOND

There are some places beyond the place we are,
places we have been to together in other pasts
down other different possible differences. Take the one
where we met for the first time and decided to be crazy together
and take off there and then for Vienna.
Arrived in the late evening, the rain tapped a scherzo
on the shiny flagstone *Straßen* while the old zither player,
left behind from a film that never got made there,
played for coins in a doorway and no-one ever heard of him
or his tune. Consider the Ferris wheel, still for the night,
and our clanky tram on its final run of the day for Mozartplatz.
We drank intense coffees there and ate those curious little sponges
that stuck in my teeth. You made me go to the splendid,
baroque lavatory to rinse my mouth before you'd even kiss me
again, which I did and you did. As we walked and held each other
dry between the sheets of rain, your shoe came off
so I warmed the wetness from your foot with my hand;
I said I felt happy to be doing that. We fetched up
in the train station waiting room with its cast-iron gas fire
and its brass door handles that said:
we are the handles of an old imperial power.
There was just that one man sitting there, his beard cut
in the *Romanoff* style. We called him Freud *entre nous* and perhaps
it even *was* him in that world – and who's to say? He was so intent
on knowing our whole story, on unearthing how exactly
we had come to be there together at that precise time,
why, of all things, we had taken it upon ourselves to go there
and why we smiled at his questions and kept on smiling.

BREAKAGES

There is a short film of Garbo,
somewhere in the reels, the rushes,
the preserved monochrome that no-one knows about,
somewhere in the last cabinet that Doctor Caligari
would ever look in, right at the back,
seared in black and white, in which, unawares,
she throws her shoulders into laughter, the sky goes dark
and all the glasses on the drinks table go to pieces.

I know this because I have seen the remake
as you look across at me when I say that you
could be a big-screen idol,
postmodern Ninotchka, and you laugh
with a laugh that could put broken glass back together again,
if you wanted to, that is; I wish I'd never met you.

MY GREAT GRANDFATHER'S
GRAVEPLATE AT GESTINGTHORPE

Not a stone, but the type of wrought-iron
        graveplate they favoured hereabouts,
and maybe only hereabouts, in those days. Since
        way before DOMESDAY
BOOK they/we perpetuated our moniker
        nearabouts. On a day before doomsday
I brook no impulse to pray into the nil, but look:
        an alien in these whereabouts.

Stood like a shadow thrown forwards in time
        who contemplates his own iron bookmark
that marks the ironic end-before-finish in what
        he was and would have gone on to be,
I'm at some edge as the plaque rusts like a
        wingless Angel of the North, sense the gravity
of this earth exert its lack as if it's trapped me
        on a ledge. Here I falter, far from the lark

of a designer in-place, with its *entrée* face,
    where our dispersal met its temporary stop,
like the MONOPOLY board boot on the Angel
    Islington square where these days I talk
the consequence of nothing and nothing of
    consequence, but once learned to walk
the hard walk, besport the two-tone Tonik
    mohair suit and perpetrate the glottal stop

that stops like a sonic vestige from the sl-slam
    of the ironmason's hammer that yammers
at me to read and read again the name engraved
    on this readymade graveplate: *John Stammers*

HOUSE ON THE BEACH

The shadows mediated by the slats of the venetian blind
stripe the silk finish ceiling;
I am reminded of the sheen on the ocean
of glossy magazine horoscopes I so deprecate,
am I not, after all, a logical and serious-minded Virgo?
Apparently, Venus is poorly aspected in Pisces
or something. I am all but nodding off at this point.

I expire across the bed with its sails full of disquietude,
its balsa-wood hull dipping and rising
on queasy unconsciousness like some *Kon-Tiki*
out to prove to me, as if I needed it,
that I am not new,
that I cannot get away from it all,
that *it* is *all* there is, and that my slumberings
retain the tell-tale signs of you
with your female body
and mouth full of explanations.
I fetch up onto this morning,
so strangely bright with exotic birds and fruit,
but still with its hoard of old stone heads.

But just how did it get here, this place –
in the margins of buying and selling
or from somewhere in the veneered wardrobe
between sharp suits, or materials
pre-weathered in the cutting room?
My new denim jacket had sand in its pockets,
that's how they distress them, you told me,
perhaps that's what the sand has done to me.
I am in distress, I had said (in body language
by rubbing the back of my neck) I am sand-blasted!

Or did it float up amongst all the debris?
It could have bobbed in at the cusp of beach and sea,
replete with the tactfully blanched flooring
and these hard little shells
that virtually stab your feet to death,
but that would be so hackneyed,
surely a place like this would be more original.

And another thing, who was it that said
don't build your house on sand?
Some old deity I think.
But rocks erode away into sand
and, like Thales said,
isn't everything just water anyway?
And he should know, having fallen down a well
trying to read the future in the stars.
And when everything is liquefied and clean,
wouldn't he be pleased, the old prognosticator,
if he himself hadn't already melted.

I strain to hear your breathing in almost the wash
of the water's edge and the lisping of the shingles
as they deliquesce into the sea;
I am asphyxiated with desire
to stroke the fine hairs of your body
and, as the sea runs over driftwood on the beach,
follow the subtle undulations of you.
I am filled up like an inflated tear
whose surface tension is so taut
that one more image of you with your poise –
your bare arms, your hands lightly crossed in front of you –
and I will break and shower into droplets like the waves
as they smash into the old wooden tide-breakers
and annihilate themselves in the air.

WHERE IS THE REST OF MY HORSE?

As I walked out my feet across
the wild green Brecon Beacons, 'O
for a big calm horse with black eyes
and a back as broad as the saddled hills ahead,'
I said. 'This is not for me this perambulation,
all is blister, soreness and rub.'

Later, after more walk, I came across,
by the path, an elder branch so wrought by growth, O
and nature and chance, that to my eyes
it was nothing less than the front leg of a horse. Ahead,
endless venomous miles of the viper ambulation
and not a ride to be had the rub.

Whilst the horse's foreleg I'd come across
was so flexed by force and the spirit in it that I said, O
where is the rest of this fantastic creature? So that my eyes
may travel its broad haunches, nape and a head
like Bucephalus on a long perambulation,
high and haughty, around another conquered city to rub

in defeat, still hard on the citizenry, shadows across
their faces, blood burning in their tired feet. O
how I figured him, my charger, in my eyes,
his great frame casting over me and me a head
full of horse and not force-marched into this perambulation,
but home rode on him to his stable, water, feed and rub.

IMPRESSION

There you are in the headlights
on that January late-afternoon in the park.
You are on one leg scraping the dogshit
from your shoe, the collar of your big grey coat up
and leant back against the trunk of the plane tree
to steady yourself.
I have put on my lights so you can see
what you are doing.
You simply noticed the smell
and stepped back out of the car to remedy it,
like a good mother must have done
many times with the kids.
These tender expertises are foreign to me.
How unlike the usual sort of date
where neither one of you wants to say anything
about those quotidian embarrassments;
I feel I could fart in front of you
and you would just say
Silly boy, or something wonderful.
I can't bear how beautiful you are there,
like a Degas ballerina,
still scraping, with the occasional grin
to let me know how you're getting on.
This picture at least, is all mine
and, for the moment, entirely licit –
look at your smile, doesn't it shine! –
and the evening is falling.

¿QUE PASA?

There is a little of everything in everything
ANAXAGORAS

Lavish rays of the flagrant sun cascade on the esplanade
or coruscate the way H_2SO_4 does, spilt on a lab floor.
A grey (or ash) acacia sweeps a sombrero from its head
making like a *ranchero* on a talcum-white *caballo*
that clops along in the shower of solar-wind particles
whose slavish job it is to bombard the Earth from space today –
Hombre, esta muy bueno aqui, muy, muy bueno.

The terracotta soil of the area merely expresses
the downright red of an Andalusian hemipode,
its feathers drenched in henna,
or a post-nuptial bedsheet doused in chicken blood
that threatens a reprise
of the madness aria from *Lucia di Lammermoor* –
you know the one where she comes out
with it all spattered down her front
and gets into *Eduardo! Eduardo!* and all that,
Eduardo! Eduardo! and all that.
You would rend the nails from your fingers
with the beauty of it, those exquisite trills
embedded in gothic death.

                              It's that even here,
here in the epicentre of a chilli enchilada,
the ice cubes in the glass hold out against it,
little visitants of the cold realms.

THE WOLF MAN

'Instincts and their Vicissitudes'
SIGMUND FREUD – TITLE OF ESSAY (1915)

It was years ago now, you understand, and I really can't recall the
    details of what we talked about. But I seem to remember that
    always was the case,
even then. You couldn't know what a thing it was in those days,
    the cafés were full of it, the talk all of psychoanalysis:
    the mind a thing to be palpably operated on
like a limb. And dreams, the talk was all of the meaning
    of dreams.

For myself there had been for some time – how shall I put it? –
    certain difficulties of a personal colour. As a young man I had
    already undergone
a number of various interventions which wouldn't now pretend to
    the epithet *medicine*: the straps, the electrodes, the vials of
    putrid liquids introduced
into my mouth prised-apart by the unspeaking orderly.
    Nothing worked.

In the end, beyond the end of their wits, as you say, my family
    sent me to him. He said he could help me if I submitted to a
    course of treatment;
a talking cure he called it. Each day I would go to his house. He
    would sit where I couldn't see him, which was important,
    he said.
And talk I did; I disclosed to him my dream.

The royal road to the unconscious, he liked to say. But to me
it was such as you might see as a small boy in a
fairground booth,
your head beneath a black sheet, peering at a magic-lantern
spectacle of horlas and ghouls, too afraid to move,
too entranced to shut your eyes.

It was this. I saw seven wolves sitting on seven branches of a tree;
slit, fixed eyes, looking not at me, but into me, as if they
were trennels
driven into my very flesh and thereby into my nerves, my brain,
my cerebral cortex. All this they achieved by just looking
and looking.
I told him my nightmare and the rest of the excrement that
surfaced from the sewers of my dreams – my predilections,
shall we call them?

All this went, for which, when you write it, you must stress I am
most thankful. Today I wear a frock coat with a modest
stock and pin, have a good wife
and even, from time to time, contemplate allowing her a child.
I work; the Bolsheviks took the estate. I like to think of that
as an especial boon in view,
as you well know, of what that old storeroom holds for me.
I attempt to do nothing *over* much.

Nowadays I have another dream. I am lying back on my long,
    rug-strewn, Egyptian couch. I turn and look
    behind me.
There are seven grey-bearded men who sit in seven large
    armchairs and peer into me. But then they are seven
    coachmen who throw back their heads,
laugh and cry out, *The royal road! The royal road!* Sometimes,
    I must tell you, I take a trap out into the woods
    at dusk, sit until night
    has spread its cloak over the trees, then wait for the yellow
    eyes of the wolves to appear.

STUCK

Alonso is more than fond of a substance that sticks stuff
to itself and anything else it touches. It's that wobbly sniff
that gets him going off for a stroll along his living room
carpet's foggy pattern like it's some kind of *jardin de plaisir*.
Right there, in that yellow soup,
it's as if *gloop* is his favourite word.
He can't get as much of it as he'd like,
and he gets enough to total a vanload of home improvers,
it must be said. His next of kin is now the Formica
that this shit is designed to stick to counters.
It's not what you might think of as Do It Yourself.
Mind you, he does do it to himself.
He can't let go: can you imagine the ripping sound,
the really loud ripping sound?

ON YOUR LAST EVENING TOGETHER

You would reach down the white mouth of the fridge,
squeeze your arm past the hardening taramasalata,
beside the unwise Gorgonzola,
for that half-drunk bottle of old Oz plonk
that he acquired at some gig or other
and had presented with a flourish.
You'd sit and talk all night
about stuff you hadn't for many a long yonk
and say again how people had often taken you
for brother and sister.
Like the time Lenny had got pissed and silly
and said you weren't made for each other,
you *were* each other and everyone had laughed.
But you wouldn't want to laugh,
because laughing might disturb something,
split some delicate membrane
that was holding back a kind of enormous pressure,
like a pent up head of water, maybe.
This is how it would be, you'd told me,
but about how it was the next day that stared blankly back.
He'd look at you with that face you'd know,
but as if distorted somehow,
in a sort of misshapen mirror perhaps,
and something in you would, at last, give way.

                              But, in the end
he'd simply gone off on his own that evening,
stayed out all night clubbing or raving or whatever,
came back in the early morning still buzzy with the drugs,
crashed straight out with a *Bye then!*,
never turned you that look, never let you
dissolve into the end of it, or say it's finished, ended,
life is now exactly different and this is after.
So what was that face you saw in the distorting mirror?
It was your face, wasn't it.

THE UNDERLINING
OF THE HEMISPHERE

The underlining of the hemisphere of your breast
sits emphatically in the palm of my hand.
Your skin's fine texture, admixture
of milk and blood, electricity and saline,
presses down against my fingers.

Still as we are, silent as the afternoon is,
the atmosphere is prickly with an aerosol
of charged particles that have passed between us.
If I was a reticulate snake, perhaps, I would lick
our odour from the air above the bed
my tongue flicking in and out, out and in,
the pattern of my skin fired up,
now yellow, now orange on black.

A general semi-light filtered by the blue blind
lies on bed and skin equally. The big slate-grey makers
that rolled their downpour over us
have messed the air and now are spent.
We are swaying, swaying a lot, not in space,
but in some kind of curvature of the spirit
where are reflections – the down along a forearm,
your breath, the warm pallor of your body beside me –
all aspects, perhaps: arm, light, torso;
we lie together and are joined;
I hold your breast, its secret.

THE CLINIC

Vivid teenage girls with awkward boys
jig about and giggle; the little radio bleats.
Everything is poster bright:
Free Condoms, Folic Acid.

You are wearing black as usual;
your black hair, your pale skin.

The salmon-red polyprop chairs sit
like strange plastic organs
from a third-form biology lesson:
And this is the oviduct or Fallopian tube,
and this is the placenta, and this is the vagina.

One girl shows a leaflet to her boy,
'That's the coil, it's for rude boys like you!'
She leans, chuckles; he squirms in his trainers,
they seem to be ceaselessly dancing, these kids.

The white of your skin,
the dark rings under your eyes.

The receptionist ticks off
a row of boxes on a sheet,
'First the nurse, then the doctor,
then the nurse and the doctor together,
then we finish off with the counsellor.'

Your eyes are fixed on nothing,
you are thinking of nothing perhaps
or of what nothing is
and when it stops being nothing.

TESTIMONY

You guided me through Dublin and Derrida
and I went along with you though you told me
that one could not be 'wrong' or 'right',
that these were 'words'. You stressed
there was no such thing as *the* canonical text,
nor even the next best thing. You drew me
into Bewley's Oriental Café standing cloned
in its own postmodern pastiche
and Grafton Street. There, over sticky buns
interpolated with glacé cherries that put red imprints
into the buns' white substance, you somehow
de-conjured up the self-styled 'writer' of the *Codex Ulysseus*
so that when he put in a radical failure of appearance
you were able to sever any connection
between author and *oeuvre*,
'What is it, after all, that is *authorised*?'
you said, and gave an allusive nod,
with your feathered black fringe and Irish-blue eyes,
to Althussar while continuing to assert
recondite doctrines through unpursed lips
pinkened with cerise so that I tumbled
head-long into ideological concurrence with you:
I knew what you were talking about and I didn't care.

From there we pursued a line of argument
along the General Post Office where I read the proclamation
In the Name of God and the Dead Generations
leaded into the brass plaque beneath Cuchulainn
and I inserted an interpretative finger into bullet holes

typed there on the wall in belt-fed lines:
the beautiful stone, the terrible queerness
of just standing there with the paths the bullets had taken
passing right through me. So we were pleased
to walk the free streets and follow
our merely quodlibetical ratiocinations
in the sight of dead heroes and live tin-whistlers.

But, when we crossed the singular Trinity quad
and perused the Book of Kells
etched for ever on the stretched skin
of unknown dead sheep, I felt a revision begin.
There were its principal letters lit up
like O'Connell Street on Paddy's Day night
knocking seven bells out of itself
fiddling and chanting and beating the bodhrán
to the infinite glory of God
and the resurrection, its parchment grey
from multifarious eyes draining the light from it
in rays, surveying its apostolic dogmas inscribed there
by quills snug against ink-stained finger calluses,
the nibs screeching like peewits
against the manuscript's interface, relentless,
taking pains and decades
to give the work the full weight of God's law.

So it was that I saw two sides of an antinomy take hold
and go to undo me like a zip.
And I saw that it was writ
that we should be the critics of our own juxtaposition,
to de-construct what there was between us
and discover if it was all just so much periphrasis
or something more.

Therefore when we found ourselves
beneath the spiral staircase at the hub
of the circular bookshop, in Tomes St,
I think it might have been, with the steeped
banks of shelves in aisles that receded
on all points of the compass
like the world itself, I delved
into the shelf labelled *Poetry / Irish / in English*,
came up with *The Collected* of yer man,
unread and silent, straight from his tongue,
which I held out to you and you took hold of
so it spanned our two hands like an arc of electric
that cracked and spat between us –
both wanting to let go, each unable to.

THE PARTY

for AN

Inured to the *Zildjian* and the percussive slant
of the small talk's charivari, we stand
and watch the sunset's hectic rant –
the snow-caked roofs colouring in bland
submission. The well between the blocks beneath
beckons, confounds our flight
from the casement in its teeth:
we will not wing it till sunrise – Peter Pans right
at the brink, wanting only the stage-wire
of our own conviction. My friend,
we stand and look and look and look and tire
ourselves out on wry asides till in the end –
our well-turned epithets, our braggadocios,
your high-blown invective – we simply nod and frown:
two minor emissaries from Boccaccio;
nightfall brings the curtain down.

Changed, all changed in our retelling of that night
when, dressed for the fray, but not yet called, furious –
before it all went right –
we gave hell its final chance with us
and took the place by storm:
                              berserkers leaping off the side,
down into our last, big mistake
and, as our feet clatter the alien tide,
screaming what we had come to take.

LIGHT

à MCR

At six o'clock, precisely at our usual time,
                    I thought of you out of a clear blue mind,
as I looked from the *Costa de la Luz* at Africa
          and felt its depth like a great dark heart.
To one side of the horizon, the white nose
          of a little red boat blipped interminably
into the sea, making no headway, so it seemed,
          across that mad panorama of enamelled ocean
with the light off it piercing the eyes
          with luxurious needles; here the sea is this blue.

All the miles of road and air and water that I'd gone through
          and over from where you are
to here, all that motion that welled up in the swell
          that rose and broke here on the shore
when this pellucid hour descended on me like a bell
          that struck six chimes and the time was six,
our six, hour of my session, it would be, with you;
          and all the individual six o'clock hours I'd passed,
all those thought thoughts spoken (an ocean of them
          as large as the continent itself, it felt like,

and larger as I'd lain there staring at the off-white sky
        with the meandering crack like the Tagus
and the cornice with the split in it, the perimeter
        of where I came to you in the commotion of me
with my soft boy's psyche, without form and nascent,
        where *J'ai sauté en les bras du ciel*)
were far from this corniche, this sweep of cliff
        and beach, this scimitar of the Moors, their
minarets and wells and geometries set in decorated tiles,
        the lucid heat reminiscent of Tashkent

in which the red boat has come on apace. It's made,
        I now see, like a middleweight, its deep chest,
its prow, its face set to the sky in leaps, falls back each time,
        but is held and buoyed up by the sea
and in this way it makes its way. So now this hour – the hour
        of my devotion, really, to you, the whiff
of Lux soap off the hands, the flux of cashmere
        with hair tied up above: Mary, mother, magus –
the light meets the atmosphere and alters it as it does;
        this air I can see through is also that blue.

SO WHAT DO YOU DO
ON YOUR WEEK OFF?

You fly to LA.
You hire a 1957 *Pontiac Bonneville* convertible.
You buy an old dog called Beaujolais.
You buy a twelve bore,
two cans of *Diet Coke*,
a packet of *Super-Codex* tablets
and a double-pack of Trojan unlubricated condoms
(for those who prefer an unlubricated condom).

You drive down Interstate 5 and across the border.
You get to a little place called *Veleidad del Mar*
meaning fickleness or whim of the sea.
You step into a bar called *Garcia's* –
motto: *Muchas Gracias en Garcia's!*
In a corner a caballero strums an indolent 12-string guitar
with eleven strings,
makes a kind of choking noise now and then.
You buy an *agua con-gas* with a slice of lime but no ice.
This is because the icecuber was lifted around this time last year
and there's no electric anyway.
You are served by a chiquita called Concepción
who is wearing a drawstring top,
the neck decorated with tiny red roses.

You talk;
you get friendly;
you discover you share the same views on many things;
you go upstairs

and after some dallying
and after some shillying and some shallying
you make *El Toro!* or The Bull!
which is a shape that can only be made
by two people who have discarded the convention
of being separate entities for the moment.

Nonetheless, and here the careful tourist should note,
she will, in time, forget you and at length
marry a tall friend of her cousin's who is a sound fellow, but who
doesn't make her laugh that jaunty, bitten-off *ha ha!* of hers.
Some years after she will give birth to a strangely pale boy-child.
She will name him Juan for a reason she can't explain,
but everyone else will call him *Juan II.*
He will grow up to become the leader of a small band
of Anglo-Mexican separatists
who will meet their various deaths in the early spring of 2031
during a ferocious but ill-fated attempt
to establish their own homeland
with its capital as the Alamo singing:
And did those feet in ancient times . . .
in Spanish which is:
Y los pies en l'antigüedad . . .

But that's for then.

You awake five days later with the worst headache since Jael
gave Heber the wake up call.
You take six of the *Super-Codex*
dissolved in the contents of the two cans of *Diet Coke*
containing phenylalanine,
but you're not a diabetic, so that's OK.

You say goodbye to sweet Concepción
with a kiss while she sleeps:
Adios, mi amor!
Which means:
Goodbye, my love,
I have loved thee well and passing deep,
but I have business in my own country
which brooks no tarrying.

You go outside;
you shoot the dog with the twelve bore
because he's old and he's just had the best week of his life
and he wants to die happy.
You bury him,
you break the twelve bore across one of the many local rocks,
make it into a cross with the barrels as the upright
and the handle as the crossbeam.
You write on the handle:

Beaujolais RIP
With best wishes
No more bitches
No more itches

You drive to LA International;
you drop off the *Pontiac*;
you fly back home.

Same old same old.

I PUT AWAY MY EARS

I put away my ears last night
as you sat and played on the Festival Hall stage.
No rock, nor roll nor R&B riffs indeed
will be needed to stifle the sad complaints of drudgery again.
You have once and for all, all and for once,
laid them down by the river
(Thames that is). Lou, I said, you
are just the contemporary icon I can but look upon
with my semicircular canals a-blazen with waxen action,
flaming up my whatever nerve, ganglion or dendrite
takes it to the dead centre of my brain at the intro to *Sweet Jane*.
So I shouted out loud in the august post-war laminate
of the auditorium: I have put away my ears tonight,
never to get them out again, and have swooned to deafness
from which, I think, there is no come-down.

ASPECTS OF KEES

Kees at the keyboard, tickling the ivories,
licking the black and white keys
with his fingers, groans out semitones
of improvised tunes (a kind of blues
or trad jazz on luminol)
in the back room of some dead-and-alive hole.
Kees booming out gloom music
into the choking, half-filled room,
the smoke and motes rising,
loom like notes in a minor key.

Kees action painting in the studio.
Kees daubing; Kees marauding the room
with off-colour hues: maroons
and grey-blues. Kees scraping the canvases
like keys screeched across the paintwork of a *Pontiac*.
Never mind the Pollocks –
Kees needs to make the paint accede
to his own creed of randomly thrown tone.
Kees succeeds in recreating his inner unease
in these expressionistic friezes.

Kees posturing like Robinson at the Keys,
i.e. Edward G patronising Bogey in *Key Largo*.
Or again as Edward G playing – can you believe it? –
Keyes in *Double Indemnity*,
and Fred MacMurray draining his confession into Keyes'
dictating machine says,
Keyes, the guy who did it was me,
I did it for Phyllis (Stanwyck) *for her kiss, see?*
Keyes sees and – how could it not be? –
Kees seeing Keyes seeing.

Kees slamming the typewriter keys.
Kees x-ing out words, cursing at his absurd,
purposeless verbs; zips out the dead sheet
from the roller. Kees mumbling, blocked,
failing once again to budge the tumblers in that seized lock,
turn the key. Kees fumbling
with the caps lock, humbled
by the just-typed sheet that says:
Kees, you're no Keats, you couldn't write a line
if your life depended on it. Kees wondering.

Kees at the Golden Gate. Car keys
in the ignition of Kees' car, they are
turned a half-turn, maybe even leaving
the nifty, little fifties radio tweeting out:
I left my heart in San Francisco . . .
Kees leaving his car in San Francisco.
Kees strolling out onto the bridge,
the tumblers finally falling into place,
something, at last, swinging wide open.
Kees leaving through it.

THE TELL

You got out a photo-album from the old days
the day you threw your fortieth birthday party.
There was you looking like your own X-ray,
women we rued not having slept with,
or having slept with, and everyone had hair
and one or two ghosts grinned out at us from their lives.

Then a couple of us two;
the first: you pulling me to you,
your lips pursed out to me in a curl,
me, eyes looking up in a demur,
eyelashes like a coquettish girl's;
the second: giving each other a big kiss.

And then this: someone saying in my ear,
You want to get rid of those.

Remember the time we saw *House of Games*
and Joe Mantegna tells the woman about the *tell*?
Then later he says to his con-men associates,
'She boosted my lucky pocket-knife!'
I asked you what *boosted* meant.
'*Stole*, it means she stole it,' you said.

I looked at those two men kissing sixteen years ago
and, do you know what, amigo?
I boosted those two photographs.

THE LAST VAMPIRE

The last vampire who took his work seriously
retired in nineteen forty-five.
He said that, in the age of the atomic bomb,
everyone was already walking dead anyway
and that a little bite here or there scared no-one.
He now lives in Eastbourne next to an old folks' home.
He likes to watch their pale wrinkled fingers
pour tomato ketchup on bacon and white bread sandwiches
and think about the old days;
he lies in a steamer chair and dreams of necks.

CERTAIN SUNDRY MATTERS

for M.A.M.

Inasmuch as you have ever heard a cowbell
extol the mountains that roll under the cow
that's wearing it, then the morning I most readily recall
was on the *Col d'Aubisque*, the mist in the valleys
like pale milk vapour from the *café complet*
we hadn't had and undulating through them
and over the ungulates,

whereas we, being right at the top then,
or over it possibly, when we came to a stop
on the apron of gravel that spread itself out
onto the roadway, and was not like an apron
at all really, in front of the old auberge
from which that girl recited *le petit déjeuner* for us,
her smile as sweet as apricot preserve
in the morning, then you too may recall
the butter, absolutely white without salt,
was a single marble bar

so that the saw'y knives scored lines on it
back and forth and yearned for something to divert them
from the ruts they themselves made, poor knives
born, when hot, to slide through it like lovers
go through their days, but, being cold and all,
only able to scrape the surface,

so that nonetheless the air itself
was invisible as usual, but I longed
to feel its hands again on my face in a caress;
so that I said, 'The hills are alive
with the sound of mooing';
so that 'John, don't be a bloody fool,' you said,

and given that her *petit ami* burped up on his velo,
de rigueur on that eructating conveyance,
his red foulard *de trop*, I thought, at his throat,
and that if it all could have been just a bit more *noir*,
or *nouvelle vague* even, we might at least
have essayed to stay up there;
but that not being the case we bid them
the long *au revoir*, the atmosphere thin
and unable to sustain us any longer in those reaches;
we had come as far as we could,
or perhaps a little farther

and insofar as we started the road down together,
heading for the Horizon
(which was the car not the sierra,
which was the mountains not the car)
and it took us these years to get down from there,

thereby did we arrive separately.

THE INFANTA OF CASTILE RIDES OUT
WITH LEOPARD, PARROT AND MANDOLIN

On the back of her great pachyderm, accompanied by acolytes,
the child-princess of the extended Castilian hegemony
waves at peons and sucks orange segments dusted
                                             with castor sugar.

Her elephant passes through the eye of the castle's portal,
nods languorously, his trunk,
made of rubber to the modern eye,
creases as he raises the prehensile nostril
to deal with a bluebottle
that has shone its blue-green carapace
across the face of the Cid and his horse's bronze mane.
The nose despatches
two hundred and fifty million years of evolving.
The white leopard regards the parrot;
the parrot clacks its beak with a clacking sound.

The Infanta encourages the mandolin player with a pig:
'Play up, play up, Emilio, today is a day for song!'
'As all days!' responds the *mandolinero*.
The *leopardo blanco*, in its snow-line raiment,
handles the heat with mere *nobleza*;
its tail undulates like the mountain roads above the city.
Our *princesa* hums her most favourite ballade,
sublime and orangey, with her orange-dyed lips,
child godling of the orange city –
the thrum of the mandolin, the clack of the parrot
as it sees itself seen in the eye of the leopard.

39

FEET

Lana deals with feet all day. They say that Lana
can tell a person's demeanour or humour
by the length of the middle toe. She reads their whims,
the shade of soft furnishings they favour in their homes,
their taste in high art (Picasso or Matisse, Ingres or David)
in literature: whether it's Scott Fitzgerald or Henry James
that does it for you (and what that 'it' exactly is)
or the one who has something of both
and whose name she can't recall –
Ford Madox Ford, that was it. And if it were Ezra Pound
stopped in Campden Hill Road on his way up
to see the great man in his stucco abode, she would know him
by the slight favouring of the right foot over the left
or the cleft of the metatarsal bones.
She can count, they say, anything about you in this way,
so why should *Cantos* be any different?
Lana, Lana, pumice these heels of me and soothe my corns away.
I wish one day you'd look up, my foot in your hand
    and say,
'You will write one hundred and twenty. This I have read.'

LISTENING TO HIS RECORD
COLLECTION WITH RODDY LUMSDEN

Slimboy Fat is playing the air grand piano,
as the chords of the waltz of the damned
mount, gather, then explode down the corridors
of memorability. 'How does he do it?'
he says, 'how does he . . . *get* you?
Is it the minor chords, the diss- or the ass-
onance, is it the hiss of the DAT
or the three-beat time signature? –
<u>one</u> *two-three,* <u>one</u> *two-three.*
P'rhaps it's that, p'rhaps it's . . .
I don't know. I woke
from my pit one night, you know,
with this going off in my head:

I'm never gonna know you now,
but I'm gonna love you anyhow.

and so forth. I've got a cassette here:
it's me singing early '80s Pulp.'

He slots it in; it is *La Soubrette* for the now,
the *Je ne regrette rien* of here and now,
somewhere between laugh and shout,
a miniature, male Piaf standing in a tin bath
a zillion miles away.
His voice takes my hand, soft –
its sweet attack, its give and capture.

'I'm nineteen on this,' he says.
As innocent as Gene Vincent
spirogyra-ing to his death
singing, *Be bop a Lula*,
his head lambent with hair oil
in his fiery rapture.

                    He is saying:
I have come a great way to tell you this;
I have been to the heart of the reverberator,
the d-d-d of the delay,
I have notes from the other side of harmony that go
shee-shee, da-da da.

Only the lonely
can know the euphony of Roddy;
only the lost will hear the dolors
in the back of his throat
that he is unable to keep in
but flow out of him like candyfloss
spun from a machine – its ambient glamours.
Where have you been all my lives,
old man in a young man's age?

I can still hear your voice singing,
Woe-woe a yay-yay,
my hyperchromatic baby.

TORCH

On a tree by a river a little tom-tit,
Sang willow, titwillow, titwillow
W.S. GILBERT, THE MIKADO

We, down High Holborn, and full up with libretto, home,
after *The Mikado*, loped.
No place – no matter how imperious
your impersonations do sound, O you,
with your impeccable Nanki-Poo –
to try to local-proper-noun pronounce,
if local you not be; especially so in your oh so *la di da*
(onomatopoeia, etcetera etcetera). I said,
'O how you do roll that O
down in your . . . your lovely . . . your lovely white . . .
and/or lollygag that L.
"Hoe-bn" is all, rest assured, you require of this word
and all you need to know of the next
par-if it's Holborn again, that is-*enthesis*.'
The synthesis of this thus and so is my
'Split a viaduct or twain?' You say, 'Shall we?'
I say, 'My point entirely, just so, rest assured, let us go . . .'
Ergo, over the jollywell in a slow and courtly,
but not so much so as to, we swankywell (my emphasis).

It is a written fact that the courtiers of the Emperor Ho
would burn feathers of the egret
to ward off demons, traitors and demonstrators
of halon fire extinguishers
(which they, of course, invented

43

many declensions before the rest of us
along with the retractable hoe,
Ovaltine, made with real ovals, and *very old* gingham)
and is where the myth of the fire-breathing dragon
is said to come from, if you follow Van Rympt.
Or they would, once a life, light chaffinch down
to mark the stolen, or half-inched, as they almost felt it, love
they had taken from the world as if from the air.

We were only twenty-four minutes from Tulse Hill
when you swept me, sweet you, just precisely off my trolley.
My one regret –
no regrets being off the menu for me and you –
is that our *belle nuit* (*nuit de la vie!*) of tripping the light
corybantic started but there and not in some continuity
we were even then enjoying it in
where I would stop and say:
You, Lady Yum-Yum, O wonder done up in a conundrum,
allow me to express my constancy in a low bow
and my adoration for the consummate sweep of your eyebrow,
my epithets heavy with cathexis.
For, when all's done and dead, regret's just an egret
with a spare consonant,
trilled through a narrow, say, aperture
by, er, perhaps (*Aarrrg!*) a sparrow. Sorry anyway.

All I can say, with my merely adequate tenor
and *Handbook of Light Opera*, is umm . . .
O take this smouldering sparrow feather I have lit
as a sign, a symbol of my whole,
my whole and contemporaneous,
as I pull down quills of fire from the air along Holborn.

44

SPINE

The mackerel sky elides lackadaisically across my eyeline,
its backbone drawn in light;
I enter beneath its shimmery gather.
The Kik-steps know me of old:
I have the bare-arsed cheek to sit on them
when the assistants aren't looking.

I have come for my self-appointed appointment:
I want to point out a point.
Anything will do,
anything will do so long as it's Love,
so long as it's Love and Poetry. I ask for
A Scandinavian Book of Love Poems
I need to show her, you see, that Love
is also a form of esoteric lament from Norway
held in the hand of a stranger.

I run my index-finger along its stiff little side,
the crypto-Nordic jacket:
ox-blood interbled with burnished bronze.

Down she steps, her dark denim skirt,
hip and leg and serendipitous slink.
I watch the receive and flex of her spine;
she lowers her eyes to the open page:

She is darker than the North star shines,
the raven that flies amidst the snow-topped pines.

WHEN I' THE NIGHT

after William Barnes

When i' the night I mind my lov apprwoch
This couch which oft we shared unslept avore,
I sieze to me a vicious self-reprwoch
That I, be'en green and näif and so therevore
Scarce to ken what unusual sight
I became to tret in her visage,
Betook, and all, a specie of inside fright
Thereby turned mine from, so joie, marriage.

Then take I as – as I have sometime seen –
The fretten brock to scrabble at his set
And violent attak his own dear pleäce;
Or Menalases who, deprivèd of his queen,
Bark'd full martial fleat vor sake of re-get
The singual consolation of her feäce.

STELLA

You wanted to live in a geodesic dome
by Buckminster Fuller. Through the skylight's fractive lenses
of our polyhedral home,
we could spectate on the very axes
of the universe, you said,
the blue entropy
of the heavens falling away from us as we lay
like two androids in the white spaceship of our bed,
the local star-chart developing in the darkroom
of the firmament – Polaris and Proxima no nearer, in fact,
to each other than I am,
now, to you or the constellations
that rain down cancers on our heads
in their serio-emissions –
all that live amidst all that dead.

Once, before physics recalled you into the black,
you whirled round the white-carpet lounge
in a freeform fandango,
your ghost thrown up by the tablelight's orange
glow, your long hair, your dippy farrago,
your bare feet tiptoeing a Pentangle
track, the woollen fingers of the carpet
intimate between your toes, the skirl
of your silken dress in a widening flirt
as you spin, spin, spin and spin –
and what does the world do but spin?
I watched you till all the clocks went bong,
the spring stopped and everything
wound down for ever.

Out here tonight, the pulsars click their half-lives
in the interstices of my blinks – so much time I never
saw out there, just the insides
of my own eyelids. I waver
on the decking of our world inside a sphere and trace
the points of Cassiopeia;
the rain pursues and outruns itself down my face.

THE CALL

Frank O'Hara (1926–66)

The phone rings, you bend your head as if lighting a cigarette
in the wind, you wedge the hand-set between collarbone
and left side of chin and cheek. You are perhaps writing
one of your *I do this, I do that* poems and clatter away
at the contraption that looks like a WWII encryption device
but is your typewriter, while continuing to chat –
(I've always felt uncomfortable doing that,
with guilt, that is, so thank you). *Hello*, you say,
*this is a very peculiar situation, while I'm talking
I'm also being filmed for educational TV.* I notice
your lump of a nose got from boxing,
I doubt very much. Perhaps you just walked slap
into a bronze slab at the Museum of Modern Art
whilst curating (although I don't think
that's part of it) or even the plate glass
on a painting by de Kooning, or Red Grooms maybe,
as if you'd tried to plunge your face straight into it like a pool.
Your voice, through that misshapen organ, tootles out:
a beaten up old sax with a split reed and is still a little
Grafton Mass.

And I wonder what else went into you,
what those chromosomes exchanged in their mambo
to a warm Puerto Rican combo somewhere in the a.m. –
close, closer, unzipping then interlacing one with another
(they call it *Love*), your return birth from nowhere
to the New World, the American dream
turned then returned into itself like a belly button;
and there you are, the dream of a poet
dreamt in your body.
                                        Something is strange to me in all this,
seeing you contemplate the waiting page.
I want to grasp your arm, draw you out of the screen,
and ask you, in the same way the paper asked you,
for words and why you answered in just the way you did;
why it was, day after day (the voice-over is saying),
you carried on your conversation
about the signage in Times Square, love,
the cigarette smoke in the 5 Spot bar that drifted like chiffon,
art, Lady Day, and the vicissitudes of the human heart again,
and the *bal masqué* of the Avenues;
what it is about the clamorous city
in the head that will not go unheard and the placing of it
out onto the page in these extrapolated phrases:
the insistent call that you couldn't not answer. Frank,

I sit here and watch you there at your desk,
your grainy, black and white countenance trapped by light,
the tap-tap of keys, the old machine
clacking like a set of false teeth
while New York lunchtime edges its way up the carriage
line by line into sight as *A Step Away from Them*
and I listen as you lisp your poems over the phone long distance.

PERHAPS YOU HAVE DREAMS

Perhaps you have dreams of a flat in Hampstead,
of a box at the Opera each weekend,
of buying candelabras and dinner parties you'd attend.

I have, for my sins, been a denizen of a West Heath pad,
seen any number of different *Mimis* fall dead,
eaten by candlelight something light on a something green bed.

Perhaps all dreams are what someone who wants you has had
and, not being able to have you, has had what you wanted instead.